A Blackbird Sings the Blues With Laughter

Poems

by

Mat Gould

Printed in the United States of America

First printing 2012

ISBN 978-0-9855291-0-9

Dog On A Chain Press
c/o Beasley Barrenton
503 Silverleaf Rd.
Zionville, NC 28698

For ordering information or all other inquiry
dogonachainpress@yahoo.com
http://www.lulu.com/spotlight/beasleybarrenton

for contributor credits/permission see back page(s)

"Tell the Saints to sit this one out, we need fools or there will be no gold"- Beasley Barrenton

"for all of our muster and all of our lore, Humpty Dumpty can get his own ass up"- Bazzel Bumgarden

come crying into this world
full of heart and pain
jes to get us a name for the fight we give-

fire away

smuggling in the horizon with the rest of the loot
so much of such
and other stuff
be there blood on my breath
an adversary whistles across the sea
yesterday's sun is still above us
and then what
perhaps we will still have the moon
to cipher the depth of this pool in between us
here where we have anchored
trying
to
bring up the biggest of sunken ship
yet another going under
sails still set
flag still raging
hull still heavy
all bones overboard
yet for one
the captain holding on never so certain of his destination-

blood as task

we take it upon ourselves to take it upon ourselves
the dismal
the disaster
any spill is an overspill
but some deaths are just of absolute to simple necessity
I know, that is terrible
oh
tis not
or we would have never gotten here to begin with
the arc
the cross
the bomb
the ash
every last bit of it has since been strewn upon
breath buried under
prayer or thunder
be it belly or beast
we take it upon ourselves
to pull the heart out of the hunted-

from where I sit I can feel the cold wind coming in

there is rubbish on the mountaintop
left here from those whom had been here before
the sun setting
is
archaic
the storm clouds
are
a day away
I see far enough to know where I am
one leaf like a kite
falls
across
my near sight
everything beyond is gigantic
as the sky breaks down its massive exhibit-

here to be there

and the rain jes came down
a light through the middle of the night
it was enough to make me get up and take a look

along with it,
the finality of the first frozen mornings' exuberant nip
the empty trees seemed relieved

I went back to lay down
but not before tripping into the rocking chair,
you would think I knew it was there by now

and the rain jes came down
a light through the middle of the night-

unless of course

you already smell defeat burning to a smolder
face in hands
ash to wind
tears in sand
squeezing the Nile to its very rind.
a dime is two nickels
either gets you old gum
or put them in the piggy
for an old day's rum
a done day's sum.
run with the sun into the hills
where chimneys trumpet
a triumphs will
a cat in the lap
or a days' whole kill.
underneath the fat there is meat at my teeth
if it is within reach then get what there is to grab
loot the tomb
chew
on
the boom until boom go boom.
a belly full of many many moon
Orion shoots across a kaleidoscope cosmos
a star
yes,
really a silly star
drops
but it could have been everything
or more than
unless of course there was something else
and I just missed it-

I put on the tigers head and search for the hall light

one o'clock in the morning
little cat is bashing at the window
he wants out.
the wind is wholeheartedly bragging through its otherwise sluggish
jury of dormant trees
I am stupidly awake
there I am with my gut out
standing in the dark
illusion in my eyes
trying to figure this all out
hmmm
I thought I was better off
as the bona fide champion falconer of my sleeping dreamland
but this feels somehow similar
somehow reverent
I roar back at the wind
and
let the cat out-

so it is

having a look around, standing here
life giving into aberrant needs
under the sun is still above ground
and here is as far from or close to about anywhere
if not for a particular place

another day for umbrellas
another brumal sousing
sagging wires as witness

without the edge of reason
debating clarity because of a beautiful face
taking to the warmth close to her own body
the shallow bath of wet streets at these feet

there is still, it seems, a definitive cheer in the conversations
as if to say
just for now is good for now
under the sun is still above ground-

every herd has gathered under empty branches

downplaying the wrath
yep that wrath
even though there is carnage on the road
and silence in the wood.
I am listening for low flying jets
thinking
there has to be something that can be done about this
threaten large missiles
corrupt society with greasy slaughtered gristle
spreadable food
give the children fangs
tell us there is acid in the rain.
it is worse the day after
when nothing has changed
and humanity goes on as normal
continuing to answer the phone
putting quarters in the pinball
swaying to the dirge
betting that the next bomb is solely another bomb
and looking at each other
questioning the answers
while villages burn-

skipping rocks toward the convoy

walking on the rubble
so many of these any days that are jes about and could be
jes about any day
when the senses fail to recognize the certainty of curse
the bugle sounds
muffled through the smog and tyranny of industry
the tirade of commerce dispensed
gumballs are still 10-25 cents
see our future in a glass full of colorful charms
broken reeds
and a call to arms
the sweet center of explosion hastens the query
steadied in the middle of all the smoke
raising a flag for ballyhoo
above the rumpus
above the tumult
on the sky fed brink
sure as certain
sights collapse
au courant
upon war and scorn-

soup kitchen baptism

fools parade their beliefs
or a loose interpretation there of
the rest of us admit our fault
and throw candy at children
share
in
the cheer
and add in a bit of salt to spice up the darlings
all while taking notice of the peripheral imminence

cold hands on tit and ass
or cock and balls

we reach through the eyes
and pull up a hideous trench where faith has bathed for so long
ladle the porridge into the dish
see if the blessed stay amongst the rest-

the scallywags knife has a sharp handle

what do you have that is perhaps closer to the truth
the scars are just marks
not X for here is the spot
nothing more than a holy wish
and more like proof of bullshit and so what
if the world was flat such things might matter
but as it is there is a chance to get around it
maybe even over it
bury the burden
leave it as treasure
set out from the island
shoot off the cannons a few miles out
sink the whole damn trove
may the imbecile swim back
and keep what they think they need
only to lose their stead
and fail to discover anything
or even wash up without a head-

anyway

wind does not die in arms
there is a supercedent to the everything of nothingness
anything we say may not mean so much now
besides
it has taken over the poem without remand
swung back into the hands to be pushed off again
anyway
what is life really worth if we know what it is all about-

Lafayette

a sad sun shines
the cemetery ground is in a frost
I walk across an iron bridge
looking down, the water is a slow sludge.
four people sit at the station
waiting on a train
or for someone to pick them up.
sometimes there is no going home
just elsewhere-

15 stories or more

I need to take an elevator to the top floor or be it roof
so I can, again, look upon a small part of the world
to see where the lights are shining
and dwindle into a few until they don't
what are we doing with all of this light
what is it that we are really trying to see
that which happens beyond our sight
is somehow right before our eyes-

the shallow water was up to my neck

I'll take what I got
because what I can get may not be what I need
a heart that burns sinks to its knees
not quite unlike the sun in its set

a matter at hand is folded up
put in the back pocket
I'll look at it later
and decide where to hang it

now back to getting up on my feet
the sun is beating at the window
it is taking longer to come around these days
a breath is not so heavy but I can see it against a stiff morning chill
no smoke, all fire-

nature spits sleet at the calm face of resurrection

the pickles have been in the refrigerator long enough to wrinkle
and seemingly shrink into shrivel
the cat is constantly meowing at the door
she knows it is the slow beginning of winter
(doesn't she?)
it's getting to be as cold as old shit soon enough as close to already
amongst the onslaught
for certain it will grow bolder
the season
the cat
the gross pickles
the temperament itself lusting after gusto
hardened bone in throat
a thrifty warmth to validate sitting at this window
with the quickening end of day.

I chase the cat away
the pickles are still good
and I move on to turning up the heat-

for there are rats in the pigeonhole

I wasn't going to confess a love for anything
it is early Sunday afternoon
and dammit, I've been listening to jazz records on the turn-style,
flipping through books
off and on the bookshelf
Pound
Ostaijen
Gayton
Buk (I can call him that because I know his ass ya know)

this is that kind of poem
not a poem at all

but somebody can rave about it
someone else can bitch about its irrelevance
I will be responsible for my own outrage
they were not here to witness these factors
had no idea the blathering cauldron of need
would not of known a pen exploded within itself
nor that my feet are mildly sweating in my winter slippers
how paunch bellied this winters gut
or that I look up from this paper
to the blinds raised
watching birds scatter and gather at the feeder.

so
here
it
goes

seems we all love a teat in our mouth
be it by spoon, sippy cup, or a hanging suet sack
a great lavish tit

sure,
you have dreamed about them
looked at or for them from across the room
across the world
right here across this page
maybe you have stacks of pages full of them
probably, if not, simply for sport
whole sets dedicated to their very celebration
thought of them with every drink
perhaps you are in need of such with the thought of each
I
think
I
will do jes that
for there are rats in the pigeon hole.

I am full of humble solitude
now that I have done what I had set out not to do
I am marching from the house into bare sunlight
record still spinning after a precious last song
stove on for teas and soups
I will be responsible for my own power outage
I will return from the day when said sunlight is at half-mast
and I have found what there was to look for.

seems
I
can
be
not so different from them rats-

mastering the spectrum

it could've been what I was doing
standing out at the end of the driveway
staring into the bluster with a fathomless shovel in my hand
giving it an idle tossing
might as well of been a pitch fork in a hay storm
chaos is not a theory
there I am, plastered by the demands of force
an ice scraped face
a 1-2 punch
an uppercut I didn't even feel until I walked away from it
3-4 steps in
a surly heave into the thin air
missing everything.

chest flat onto the deck

there was no shadow standing over me
only brazen white light
and what I now know as an apparition's laughter-

inside the crystal ball

from the glass paintings of the same setting on the brick wall
to the foul mouthed under aged college girls sitting at the corner
table talking shit about other peoples' friends
and
the first full on blizzard of the heavy breasted fully cocked winter
right outside the basement bars' picture window
fingertip
to
lip
an immense journey into legend foretold
I put the hard plastic cup one less guzzle full of beer back on the
wooden table.

seeking nothing
the picture is taken
they are all bundled up
ready to pound the tundra
the spittle of their bragging right frozen to their face.

God be challenged with javelin and lightening
hear me roar
carrying kittens at my jowl and laceration on my chest
chasing spirits from the rubbish
and into the gust
a slobbering deity swallowing blood to boast
and washing it down with the sweat of swine.

but really
I am condonedly sitting here
inside the crystal ball
holding up my end of the deal-

a mild confession from a not so mild mannered man

speaking in the native tongue…
the quite possible is not so random
familiar to a bad tooth
a smile doan keep it from happening
one
could
be
wise
to keep a stone in their cheek
we have to grind life down into grit
or so be it I certainly have to-

we all get fat from the seed

here is the encrusted snot of electric heat
and the brittle hair of below freezing
first
of
February air
we stay inside and sort perishable from kernel
everyone hovers into the light
windows breathe just enough to exchange the elements we need
we cannot keep everything out
we cannot help but let some things in
the rodents take to their teeth and gnaw at the cabin walls-

an old trick

there seems to be no end
breath erupts
and
keeps us from death
begging
for
whatever is left-

the sporadic change-over of an evening reluctant: ode to Sandburg

snow flurry melting against the glass
a big heart igniting under an electric wire sky
doing
its
best
to reflect the pavement
a huff of roof-top steam speeds unto dissipation
a few jagged tree-tops binge out loud
if this aint the damndest of things
it must be something else-

clearing the way

some of us grow old
some of us get better with age
there is a button to push on most mornings
it does not dictate either or
but for the sake of this poem it does

I have changed my alarm clock
from a devastating siren
to the disproportionate static of talk radio
in hopes that
this makes for a better awakening

but today it took another marvelous typhoon
an upheaval that had kept me up throughout most of the night
and left me without much kick
again with slowly staggered steps
following the cats to the door
noting their pure vigor
as though they knew of exactly what they were running toward
I suppose they do

I closed the door on it
I am going to give it few
and then I'll look to do the same-

finding the essence without necessarily looking to hard unless one counts every fucking day up too now

my fingertips are dry
the lifeline on my palm crosses over one I cannot identify
this morning
on the corner
the world was beautiful
the sun was an empire
everything passing by held its strength over its own head
I kept my hands in my pockets
reaching for a force internal
I took it home
and buried it deeply under the mountain (near the garden next to
the stone swan yard ornament)
so I'll know where to find it
when I need it again-

the two ex-champions (having a hard time with the shadows)

a good poem
takes all night
even if you're not doing anything.

the typewriter has been covered up on the bookshelf
all winter
I have only looked at it a couple of times
it is as if we are separated
and doan even wanna touch
but we both need a place to sleep and be warm
even with all of the offers to go elsewhere
we stay in our corners
waiting for the bell-

raising rabbits

no giant can stay small for long
put one in the box, break neck
it went willingly to the hand
no idea if it had an idea what was to take place
for sure there was a fallacy of grandeur
a love contour that was bigger by the shade
strong in the dark
the famished coydog met in the swelter of a swamp
what few teeth it has, placed just right
accordingly
the bunny lays down
gives birth to sacrifice
who is to say which is still alive
no idea if there is any idea of an afterlife
nor if we are better off for such-

the brilliant death march of an entire orchestra in uproar

the cold and damp has lead the flies inside
their cemetery is at the window sill
and under the lamps
they have restlessly brooded themselves without submission
as if their sole purpose was to go mad
every instinct hastened for the glory of the bulb
a disturbing ritual
this intention
to
break through and illume-

flabbergasting the coward

I had walked over to the side of the house
watching two crow making the most of their racket
-I applaud the erratic dedication of all things persistent-
crashing in and out of the shrubbery
wings held high
thrashing the supposed barricade of their own resistance.

the morning had brought with itself a stilted defiance of season

I am not licking my chops
if not for leftovers there would be perhaps nothing left for meal
every creature is awaiting the egg so that we may raid the nest.

for now I tuck in my shirt
with no abounds but this verse instilled
a blackbird sings the blues with laughter-

the hard on (an ode to Spring)

a short fat dog strutting in a dead pant across the parking lot
he doan hear nah horn or whistle
he's got the heat on his peckered mind
with a blue collar tight on his neck
he can feel the squeeze at all times
but right now
there is a leap in his step
"I'm a git that bitch
any other day that bitch got me"
sniff it out, buddy
and then go git some more of it-

revenge

it
was
pouring down rain
until
the sun
came
back
out-

nude by noon

I don't know about the endlessness of anything
certainly if whatever may be is taking that long
there
is
something else to do
a stop, drop and roll
a flame throw
a swallowing of the sword
lay the jacks out on the floor and pick up what you can before the
ball comes back and bounces again
or stand naked in front of the open door
let it swing full of swagger
sing along with the sound that sounds good pronounced
there will be no holding up the day-

any days battle (continued)

I
am
looking out once more
over the hills
over my shoulder
somewhere the sun is not far from breaking through these clean
afternoon clouds.
for
some
reason
I suppose
this is what the big little world demands-

the ballad of todays' odd ballet

watching them from the far end of the terrace
I am actually only looking at them
in and out of doors
some of them holding hands
some of them with shopping bags
some of them right in and right back out.

some of them are outrageous in their beauty
darlings of the kingdom
some are fair and no doubt intelligible enough to get away with
their pout
some I pay not so much attention to
but are an epitome unto their own I am sure.

and yet others are here to be just that.
all I have made up is what I am thinking and that is not so made
up.

it is an odd ballet on this veranda
the covered air still pushing through
(I have never been to a ballet, perhaps they are all an odd occasion;
seems to me they'd be just that)
and this one is no different
but it is conjuring up a bit of idle sense.

with these windows to see through
into the intent faces on the other side
you should be able to see what you are about to walk into
but there has to be a feeling
one that comes with us
and one that we take along to talk about later
over dinner somewhere else-

the confluence: an iconoclast of verse

the coffee shop doan always work for a write
the picture window was just a window
the parking lot was drab and drizzled on
conversations were simple enough
maybe it was the electro type folk music
none the less
the bar is better
does the trick, pulls out the bunny by its ears
at 1:00 p.m. on a given week-day afternoon
where some of the patrons stayed beyond their lunch break
and the others are usually here by now anyway
there is no guessing
to
what the looks on these faces mean
it all adds up and empties into the understanding
I am not looking for the answers today
plenty of light comes through the door
every time it opens-

the bar doan always work for a write
at 1:00 p.m. on a given week-day
where some of the patrons have stayed past their lunch break
and
the others are usually here by now anyway
there is no guessing
to
what the looks on these faces mean
it all adds up and empties into the understanding
I am not looking for the answers today
the coffee shop is better
does the trick, pulls out the bunny by its ears
the picture window is just a large window
the parking lot is drab and drizzled on
the conversations are simple enough
maybe it's the electro type folk music
none the less
plenty of light comes through the door
every time it opens-

a load on the dock

the baristas' tits are about to plop out of her tube top
I doan care to see them
but sure, I'd take the quick look
a snap shot of the assault
breast swinging
faces caught
lips bit
tongues swallowed
hands at the well for a barrow of flesh
pour it on
ice the rink
baffle without delusion
-dim colored lamps overhead-
you would suck on them if they were inches from your mouth
half
of
the mass
is in its own horde
gargling and giggling
flinging the foam from their chops
blood on the bone
a moan in the throat
lunch hour is over
I have pissed around long enough
order up-

this poem

this poem
has struck a deal
with
the big word

says it will not use such

this poem
shall hang by a seemingly odd amount
of
electrical wire
on
the leaning telephone pole

this poem
is an avant-garde precipitation
condensed
as
soon
as
it reaches the ground
if not before

this poem
likes to kiss itself in the mirror
thinking it is you

this poem
can
charm your panties right off

so
read this poem as it does so

this poem
will read other poem
and
then write another poem
hoping other poem will do the same

this poem
looks at purple brick next to green cinder block
this poem sees crumbling chimney
and ragged branches
painting themselves together
into
a
somewhat
cheery yet grotesque landscape
of
oxidized gray eternity

this poem
is
standing on the corner drinking gasoline

this poem
leaves behind oil spill mandalas
in the image
of
this poems wild animal eyes

this poem
will change with time essential
or
get torn down
when
this poem
decides

this poem needs bigger words to emphasize

this poem
can always find that delicate little place
this poem thought it could hide away

this poem
is
right here-

.

just enough hooey to flatter the darling

breathe into my breast
tell me more than there is to tell
just by putting your ear against the nimble beat
you will hear everything I have to say
everything else may come off as aloof and indignant
a parity that I live with
a discussion I have had with myself on numerous occasion
better yet
earlier today
and the night before
I look forward to it being a part of existence again tomorrow
oh tomorrow, you sucker for any pretty beast
naked and raw under the cover of fluttering eyes
I may cuss such
damn the dare itself
a beauties travesty forlorn as only a temptress
a fancy bluff that only stiffens my pants
what to do now with this extravagant orchestra of thought
perhaps a reprieve
perhaps agony dulls its tusks
perhaps I let it be known
tis jes a poem
perhaps there is the universe to encounter otherwise
perhaps it has already slapped me to the punch
perhaps there is no need for any of this
perhaps
tis jes a poem
for the dearest of us all-

ever since

the night had become too much for itself
to
continue
without the first hue of the morning
we
all
miss
our
lovers
more
when we know they'll be back-

we give our bones to the sun

a carousel of buzzards
high
over the hills
while
the brick
and the brown
of
the town
is
scorched
by the late afternoon sun

we give
our bones
to
the sun
to
the sun
we give
our bones-

this is for there being nothing more than a quiet plea

under canopy as the drizzle suffocates the early summer heat
slow rock-n-roll on the radio
it is nice to stand outside and listen to the world watch itself go bye
no backs against the wall
evening has settled the days intent
our vows have carried on
we will have the truth
                           or its retreat
            by the end of a night-

there is a matter of fact in here someplace

(the lawn at the post office smelled of dog shit melting into the
awful humidity today)

there was a bee banging itself against the inside of the window at
my desk
appearing to be on the wrong side of things
what is there but to try for capture and release?
well, the obvious other

there is another thunderstorm trying not to weep
it is going to hang around for a couple of days
a fly on fresh death

I need to get these books in the mail
if I don't head into town soon I am going to get stuck behind a
school bus on its rural route
and then I will be merely sitting in my car,
I do not want to be merely sitting in the car
oddly damned at intervals

and it is exactly from there in which I am writing this-

American domestic (pt. 1)

the driest of dirt on my pink cup
a Junior Kimbrough 78 on the cut
most
of
my
gut instincts
are telling me to make a run for whatever there may be
but sometimes you gotsta stay put
get your hands up in front of your face
these are the times you swing at everything
and take the same along the way

there
is
love in the end

jes make sure you got one good eye without the swell
so you can see how pretty it be-

take it all in

a catalyst
a martyr
who cares about being either
we try to mold them into one and the same
a bomb to blame the ignorance on.

you doan have to go far and away
but if you are already there
enjoy the stay
and if you will
bring me a t-shirt
printed with the palms of the bay
as the lamp of day
burns your lovers bare ass
spread out
on
the shore
with a million salted bones
in
the smoldering sand-

spraying down the rocks

we walked down the street to watch things burn
faltering houses made of dust and mildew
a dry shambles in the southern august heat
scraped to their dwindling husk
the blackest smoke held together by the smothering aridity
it was hard to know what soot was old and what soot was new
another empty hole on this side of town
they just go up in flames this time of year
the sirens falsetto momentarily paused-

...much like morning

in my sleep I was on a river-boat
slowly counting bridges
and
noticing the few people standing on them
imagining
what they might imagine
looking out
looking from
looking over
or
not looking what so ever
as the heavy river drags along
I gamble with my thoughts
the paddle is turning
keeping the ship at a drift
less and less lights on the waterside
until
the wide shift
back toward the sturdy and evident
sight of the city
returning...

intellectual symptoms concurrent: a partial ode to Creeley

one day per day
be willing
to
deny the future
for
time being what it is
the sentence abrupt
an idiot at the podium telling us that we must

gallery open for thought

directions in a circle taking us to the other side of the street
going
back
the way we came
here to stay
for the time being present-

a tentet and then some

power lines run deep into the country
where folk doan hush their dogs
or feed their cats
seems to be a necessity
much like love or the lack thereof.

have you ever seen the moon arouse the valley from under a
thunder that is the nights protest?

in a dusk composed warbling entirety
the crickets keep their selves hidden
but sound as if they are everywhere at once-

drip beat downpour

a much needed rain
upon the mountain.

insects had taken to the under leaf
slowly chewing through.
I
stand (wimp with the wind)
upon
the threshold
under the overhang
slowly wetting my lips
the mutiny has been settled-

I am sure life is worth it

I used to work the kissing booth
it did not pay much
and there was less love than I'd thought there would be
perhaps that was my fault
because I only enjoyed a supple tonguing if she was a fair harlot
up for anything
who am I to hope for such insolence
never
the
less
I am sure life is worth it
somewhere amongst the carnival someone is winning a teddy bear-

take the derby and head for the gate

sit me down
sit me down
I need a rest
I have been jes standing around
pennies for thoughts
now my pockets are full
this would again be a good time for a bottle of something cold
I
am in-
between
getting old and staying young
I have yet to hold the rail
I keep my hands on her hips
close to the undertone

the meaning of it all
is
swatting at a bee

if we bet only on the front runner
well,
here comes The Jolly Duper
5 horses back
closing fast
with 10 lengths left-

Beasley Barrentons wit sabbatical presents Bazzel Bumgardens dismay

all the people and their fucking noise
dangerously close to the edge
it
is
because
of
the world
stop, do the contraption cheer
go poem
keep it together
ride the mercy train
is this one dimensional
or
three dimensional
right up on and coming at me
was it pure radiance
or
the moon
half-assed yet certain
every belief admires basic truths
the cat was never in the bag
the threat has always been on its knees
who the fuck are you, right?
big and on the poster
a cool iron, baby
this is not the slow love of infinity
or maple syrup on your hominy
the rigid brim
fell at the end
and now it is something different
starting again-

if the spirit moves you

huddled away from another flimsy mist
waiting out its drifting hour
giving ourselves back to another day
spring was long over and somehow the summer was in the midst of
its wither
albeit stalled
by lecherous nights having an affair with the dallying sun
lovers that must part but are holding on
they too are waiting out the drifting hour
I speak of such easily
all of this
waiting it out
waiting for what?
I am only certain of nothing so much as the drunken later-

the belligerent poem

someone else's cigarette butts are in the ashtray in front of me
the waitress isn't going to pick them up
a beer is in my hand
the waitress has been bringing them when I put an empty out
a sweet milk maid
and
this poem like any poem
is
feeling you up for the sake of us all
I'll ask it later how it was;
where were you slick where were you rough,
after a few drunks stumble on
right about the instant I'm ready to do the same
feel you up
or
stumble on-

the whimsical wisdom of wishes and wonder

adorning each other in the mad early morning
before the world takes over and slams us into oblivion
and ruin
under a perfectless sky

the cat has gone from a purr to a hiss
all we have done is look at it

a certain blaze in the gut
the heart stuck at thump
struck dumb, capered once again
behind
a
hundred stars
there
are
a hundred stars
behind a hundred stars

before you know it, it is before you know it
the molten air of the void
the spit of a swollen lip
weeds growing up warehouse walls

how do we keep beauty a secret

with emeralds in our sacks
we take roof-tops across the city
and lacquer them in the celestial glare of high noon
a rock at your window
says "let me in"
the words of a poem go into and over one another

mix my drink with your finger
and poke me in the eye
the honest bones of a long time ago
tell the story about how this all came to be-

"smells like heaven"

another one of those over-heard suggestions…
could be pussy
could be pizza
could be the sky soaking up sweat
could be the end of it all
epically everything splendidly at an end
everything on fire
dancing upon itself
with a lover that leaves the imagination to come up with its own
explanation
of
"smells like heaven"
the muck
the fume
the fuel
the one big ball going bang-

in the end there is rib without skin

the jackal are in my yard again
cock out
ass up
hovering over any hole
pots and pans won't chase them off
I am going to have to eradicate the scrounging bastards
sharpen the spear
poison the peanut butter
ready the rubber voles
and head out to the field wearing only a leather strap
and fur at my waistband

can you imagine the look on my face
I can imagine the sheer hilarity
if
not
the brief utter fear of certainty and conflict upon your snout

are you kidding me? one may ask.
I might be
but
pondering such is blunder-

might not be what you thought

life calls the shots
don't forget the spectacle of phenomena
or the pretty faces
you will need them along the way
from behind the wheel
looking out the window
that just a moment
don't forget the moon in the morn
or the steeple above the rest of the town

there is no big deal
but there is a lot of other shit
its residue in your grips

don't forget to sleep it off
and don't forget the rest of what I didn't mention.-

Mat Gould has published three other chapbooks with Dog On A Chain Press, he is not a mystery, he stays up on a hillside in Western North Carolina, keeping a close eye on the life those mountains provide and he would just as soon disregard the rest of what may or may not be. If not for the minor insistence of his work and his appreciation for those who read him he would do just that. So this is for them, this is for you, this is for him.

Above photo: Tree and Pump House: Gabriel Santerno…adopted out of Portland, Oregon into Sacramento, Ca. Now lives where she belongs in Lake County, CA via Idaho. She is a good old soul and loves her family. Dog On A Chain Press loves her and we are always glad to use her work.

Inset one: Mia Maguire: is a 21 year old model making her way in between San Diego and Los Angeles with trips to Chicago and New York for both work and personal interest. She is a vibrant fan of Dog On A Chain Press (and an absolute darling). We hope she knows how much we appreciate her.

Inset two: aficionado/soon to be published by Dog On A Chain Press…Dena Rash Guzman, a Portland/Las Vegas/Shanghai based poet/editor/performer and founder of www.UnshodQuills.com. Give her a look Dena RashGuzman.com.

Photo for Inset two by Eva Steil: Mapp and Cord Series…featuring some of the best known writers and artists in Las Vegas, her work can be found in art galleries galore and all over the world wide web.

Inset three: Photo by Stephane Lepine: Series- Anka. We asked for months, I am pretty sure we even begged. Stephane finally said "I would be honored". The honor is all ours. His work is maddening. StephaneLepine.tumblr.com.

Cover Art : Bird: Live at The Can by Jonathan Smith- Owner/operator at Shed Studios in Boone, NC. His focus is primarily on pencil work and oil painting with an occasional bit of music. He claims to have once almost been bitten by a sea snake and has a dog named Cricket. Dog On A Chain Press would like to welcome them both into our endeavors. More of his work can been seen at https://www.facebook.com/pages/Shed-Studios/121852917851907.

Dog On A Chain Press would like to raise a glass and extend a gallant praise to all of those who have hunkered down and helped us feed the hyena. We will have to make the bunker bigger and we are indeed willing to do just that. We once again invite you into "the subtle apocalypse we all dream of". Pura Vida-

*a few of these poems have appeared online and in print most notably at Gutter Eloquence and Black-Listed Magazine.